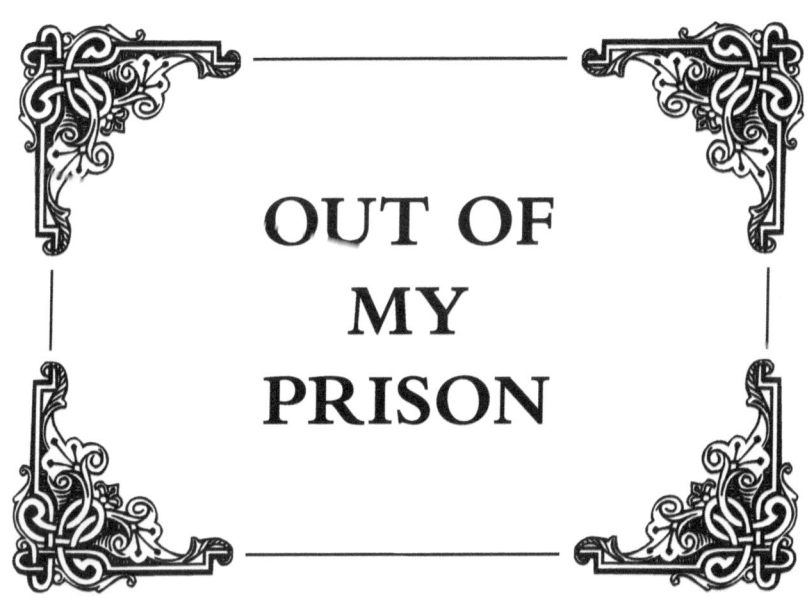

OUT OF
MY
PRISON

A POETIC JOURNEY TO PEACE

ZACH CHUTE

WESTBOW
PRESS
A DIVISION OF THOMAS NELSON

WestBow Press books may be ordered through booksellers or by contacting:

WestBow Press
A Division of Thomas Nelson
1663 Liberty Drive
Bloomington, IN 47403
www.westbowpress.com
1-(866) 928-1240

Because of the dynamic nature of the Internet, any web addresses or links contained in this book may have changed since publication and may no longer be valid. The views expressed in this work are solely those of the author and do not necessarily reflect the views of the publisher, and the publisher hereby disclaims any responsibility for them.

Any people depicted in stock imagery provided by Thinkstock are models, and such images are being used for illustrative purposes only.

Certain stock imagery © Thinkstock.

ISBN: 978-1-4497-2920-2 (sc)
ISBN: 978-1-4497-2919-6 (e)

Library of Congress Control Number: 2011918466

Printed in the United States of America

WestBow Press rev. date: 11/11/2011

For those who were there for me in my darkest time,

when I needed compassion but didn't deserve it.

Psalm 142:7 (King James Version)

Bring my soul out of prison, that I may praise Thy name:
the righteous shall compass me about; for Thou shalt deal
bountifully with me.

PREFACE

In any struggle, we face a turning point at which we can begin healing. I experienced this when I realized I could not heal without first accepting God's forgiveness. While the ultimate forgiveness I needed was my own, I could not escape my guilt without first giving myself permission to accept God's grace and then coming to terms with the fact that He has washed away my past. I learned that we need not worry about past failures, only about those we can strive to avoid in the future.

My favorite poem in this book is "You Forgave Me, So I Forgive Me". It is my turning point. I can't help but cry tears of joy every time I read it or remind myself of it. We cannot serve God as the vessels He wants us to be until we can tell ourselves we have His love, regardless of our worthiness.

The poems I wrote before my "turning point" arise from a mind mired in the turmoil of self-loathing. The poems following that point flow from the healing in my life. I have included Scripture to give hope to those poems from the darkness and comfort for those on the path of God's love. I have omitted my interpretations of the poems, as you are free to determine their meanings with His guidance in the way He knows will help you most.

This book is my attempt to help you find your turning point, because you deserve it. May God bless your journey and give you the peace that only He can.

All verses are King James Version

If we confess our sins, he is faithful and just to forgive us our sins, and to cleanse us from all unrighteousness.—
1 John 1:9

Alone

Leave me be,

I can hurt myself.

I don't need it from you.

There is so much pain.

I know I could do better,

But why do you have to remind me?

Constantly.

Incessantly.

Always. Criticism.

Wherefore comfort yourselves together, and edify one another, even as also ye do.—1 Thess. 5:11

Warranted

Maybe I deserve it.

Maybe I am really as bad as you say.

I see what should be done,

And don't always do in the right way.

So much could be better,

But must that always come into play?

If I'm trying,

Could you just be happy for a day?

Let no corrupt communication proceed out of your mouth, but that which is good to the use of edifying, that it may minister grace unto the hearers.—Eph. 4:29

Simple

I wanted them to say I was good,

But they never would.

Now they do,

But I don't think it's true.

For he shall deliver the needy when he crieth; the poor also, and him that hath no helper. He shall spare the poor and needy, and shall save the souls of the needy. He shall redeem their soul from deceit and violence: and precious shall their blood be in his sight.—Ps. 72:12-14

Inside

What have I done?

I will never forget.

How would I disclose?

I will never know.

Can I ever escape?

I will always hope.

Does anyone hear me?

I will always wonder.

Do I even care?

Maybe.

And the prayer of faith shall save the sick, and the Lord shall raise him up; and if he has committed sins, they shall be forgiven him. Confess your faults one to another, and pray one for another, that ye may be healed. The effectual fervent prayer of a righteous man availeth much.—James 5:15-16

Tremble

Are they watching me?

Are they judging me?

What do they think?

So many things I can't control.

So scared to think about tomorrow.

How will I cope?

How will I handle all of this on my own?

I don't think I can.

Where is the help?

Left behind, turned away so long ago.

Please, somebody help.

Not forsaking our own assembling together, as is the habit of some, but encouraging one another; and all the more, as you see the day drawing near.—Heb. 10:25

Not Sure We Should

The road less traveled was taken

And led to a place where none should go.

So travel the common road

And find . . . something else.

But exhort one another daily, while it is called To day; lest any of you be hardened through the deceitfulness of sin.—Heb. 3:13

Sleep

Where are you?

How could you leave me here?

To handle this zoo

Without your dear peace?

These things I have spoken unto you, that in me ye might have peace. In the world ye shall have tribulation: but be of good cheer; I have overcome the world.—John 16:33

The Judge

Sitting aloof,

On the pedestal of self-worthiness,

Quick to criticize,

Confidently inerrant.

More intelligent,

Than all he encounters.

Just ask him,

He knows it's true.

Yet when the façade is gone,

There is only the turmoil,

The inner strife,

Always berating the berater.

So much to fix within,

Just looking for a distraction.

Judge not, and ye shall not be judged:
condemn not, and ye shall not be condemned:
forgive, and ye shall be forgiven:—Luke
6:37

Justified

Prove to me that it's wrong.

You can't.

Show me why I shouldn't.

I won't listen.

If it's gray, I'll go either way.

I do what I please.

It doesn't matter what others think,

You're too sensitive.

If we say that we have fellowship with him, and walk in darkness, we lie, and do not the truth: But if we walk in the light, as he is in the light, we have fellowship one with another, and the blood of Jesus Christ his Son cleanseth us from all sin. If we say that we have no sin, we deceive ourselves, and the truth is not in us.—1 John 1:6-8

The Hypocrite

"That is wrong",

You will be told.

And all along,

The accuser is bold-

ly doing that wrong.

So when they continued asking him, he lifted up himself, and said unto them, He that is without sin among you, let him first cast a stone at her. And again he stooped down, and wrote on the ground. And they which heard it, being convicted by their own conscience, went out one by one, beginning at the eldest, even unto the last: and Jesus was left alone, and the woman standing in the midst. When Jesus had lifted up himself, and saw none but the woman, he said unto her, Woman, where are those thine accusers? hath no man condemned thee? She said, No man, Lord. And Jesus said unto her, Neither do I condemn thee: go, and sin no more.—John 8:7-11

<u>My</u> Bad

The blame was misplaced,

So far from the culpable party.

All to be done now is to say,

Hate Me

Because I know what to do,

But I don't.

Because I know how to treat you right,

But I don't.

Because I know I'm often wrong, and should admit it,

But I don't.

Because I love you more than I could ever love myself,
and want to tell you,

But I don't.

Because I do,

Hate me.

But God commendeth his love toward us, in that, while we were yet sinners, Christ died for us.—Romans 5:8

Neverm(i)nd

(i)'ll keep it to myself.

(i) can't say what (i) want,

It will only hurt you.

It's not my place

To fix what you can,

And have a right to remedy.

Don't listen to me,

Because (i) don't matter.

If any man among you seem to be religious, and bridleth not his tongue, but deceiveth his own heart, this man's religion is vain.—James 1:26

Despicable

I allow myself to

eat,

sleep,

rest,

relax,

while so many

starve,

freeze,

grieve,

fear.

And I don't seem to care.

Forgive me, Lord,

For all that I hoard,

And my lack of

Recognition for your love.

And he said to them all, If any man will come after me, let him deny himself, and take up his cross daily, and follow me.— Luke 9:23

You Forgave Me,
So I Forgive Me

I am free to be

Released from my own shame, for

You did sans request.

If we confess our sins, he is faithful and just to forgive us our sins, and to cleanse us from all unrighteousness.—1 John 1:9

Edify

One another

At every opportunity.

For a brother

Is much more likely

To bother

With your daily

Cares and concerns

If he knows that you truly

See the good in

His deeds.

Let us therefore follow after the things which make for peace, and things wherewith one may edify another.—Romans 14:19

Selfless

Forget his feelings.

He just wants to help you.

Ignore his wishes.

He just wants to help you.

Disregard his needs.

He just wants to help you.

And never fail to remember, you are loved.

Selflessly.

But love ye your enemies, and do good, and lend, hoping for nothing again; and your reward shall be great, and ye shall be the children of the Highest: for he is kind unto the unthankful and to the evil.—Luke 6:35

It Sounds Like It Means What It Doesn't

Cache some cash

'til you're sure your

Caste is cast,

And aloud you're allowed

To beat one who would do anything for a beet.

Haughtily they're discussed, and disgust

Seems to rise in the seams

Of your soulless existence, 'til no solace

You find, and in eternity fined

A sum that some

Suede cannot pay. Swayed?

Let trust be trussed

Whither it should, lest it wither

And leave you bare to the bear

Of hell. Hail God's word,

He'll heal wounds that be

Ours through timeless hours,

And wrest our worries, that we may rest,

Wrought free from the rot of sin.

And he said unto them, Take heed, and beware of covetousness: for a man's life consisteth not in the abundance of the things which he possesseth.—Luke 12:15

Offended

Are you?

Of course.

Did I care?

Of course not.

Do I now?

I do.

I am so sorry.

But whoso shall offend one of these little ones which believe in me, it were better for him that a millstone were hanged about his neck, and that he were drowned in the depth of the sea.—Matt. 18:6

HU<u>m</u>BL<u>e</u>

All are equal in His eyes.

This should be no surprise.

So let us rise,

And hear one another's cries.

For none can stand

Reliant on their own hand.

We are a band

Of peers in this land.

If my people, which are called by my name, shall humble themselves, and pray, and seek my face, and turn from their wicked ways; then will I hear from heaven, and will forgive their sin, and will heal their land.—2 Chron. 7:14

Success

Stop

Trying to do what you can't.

Stop

Trying to fix what you can't.

Stop

Trying to be what you can't.

Stop

Trying to deny what you can't.

Stop

Trying to help who you can't.

Start

Helping yourself,

And succeed.

And why beholdest thou the mote that is in thy brother's eye, but considerest not the beam that is in thine own eye? Or how wilt thou say to thy brother, Let me pull out the mote out of thine eye; and, behold, a beam is in thine own eye? Thou hypocrite, first cast out the beam out of thine own eye; and then shalt thou see clearly to cast out the mote out of thy brother's eye.—Matthew 7:3-5

Serenity

There is:

No problem too large

No tragedy too devastating

No soul too dark

No sin too incriminating

For His love to remedy.

The LORD is my shepherd; I shall not want. He maketh me to lie down in green pastures: he leadeth me beside the still waters. He restoreth my soul: he leadeth me in the paths of righteousness for his name's sake. Yea, though I walk through the valley of the shadow of death, I will fear no evil: for thou art with me; thy rod and thy staff they comfort me. Thou preparest a table before me in the presence of mine enemies: thou anointest my head with oil; my cup runneth over. Surely goodness and mercy shall follow me all the days of my life: and I will dwell in the house of the LORD for ever.—Psalm 23

Prayer

Lord, give us each day:

The strength to deny the material things of this life,

The love to wish the best for everyone we encounter,

The humbleness to know that our transgressions would be no more heinous should they be committed by another,

The wisdom to accept that we know nothing save Your revelation,

The compassion to help those who can't provide the necessities for themselves and those for whom they provide, for we would be in the same plight without your blessings so undeservedly bestowed upon us,

And the unceasing reminder that we are not given what we deserve, thanks to Your grace.

Amen

www.ingramcontent.com/pod-product-compliance
Lightning Source LLC
Chambersburg PA
CBHW050339290526
45785CB00006B/2556